THE AMERICAN SOUTH
Four Seasons of the Land

WILLIAM A. BAKE /JAMES J. KILPATRICK

THE AMERICAN SOUTH

Four Seasons of the Land

Oxmoor House, Inc.
Birmingham

Pages ii, iii, iv, v; *The Four Seasons.*
BLUE RIDGE MOUNTAINS, NORTH CAROLINA.

The American South

Copyright © 1980 by Oxmoor House, Inc.
Photographs Copyright © 1980 by William A. Bake

Published by Oxmoor House, Inc.
Book Division of The Progressive Farmer Company
Publisher of *Southern Living®*, *Progressive Farmer®*,
and *Decorating & Craft Ideas®* magazines.
P.O. Box 2463, Birmingham, Alabama 35201

Eugene Butler Chairman of the Board

Emory Cunningham President and Publisher

Vernon Owens, Jr. Executive Vice President

Conceived, edited and published by Oxmoor House, Inc.,
under the direction of:

Don Logan Vice President and General Manager

Gary McCalla Editor, Southern Living

John Logue Editor-in-Chief

Jerry Higdon Production Manager

Joan Denman Associate Production Manager

Designer: *Robert L. Nance*

LIBRARY OF CONGRESS CATALOG NUMBER: 80-80754
ISBN: 0-8487-0495-9

Manufactured in the United States of America
FIRST PRINTING 1980

Preface

If the doors of perception were cleansed
  every thing would appear to man as it is, infinite.
For man has closed himself up,
  till he sees all things thro'
  narrow chinks of his cavern.

William Blake
The Marriage of Heaven and Hell

Perhaps Blake was overly pessimistic, but the point is well made: we tend to see too narrowly. As Nineteenth Century author and philosopher George Perkins Marsh put it, "Sight is a faculty, seeing is an art." Man is not without recourse, however. Each of us, in some way, has the gift of perception and can share it with others. In this, the artist has a special place. Literature, painting, photography, and the other arts have always tended to expand the limits of human awareness. Artists exercise their role by assimilating their surroundings and transposing them through their creativity. Occasionally, art even outdoes itself by imposing something new and unique upon society.

The American South enters the arena by presenting the most encompassing visual portrait of the region yet attempted. Within these pages is a suggestion of past and present—both cultural and natural—that seeks to expand awareness of what we are working with as we mold the future. Yet the book intends more than this. The objective reality of the South is not only what is presented here; rather these pages contain a more personal view of the region: a transposition. In the image-making process, I exercise my role, transposing objective reality, and sometimes even imposing my own perception of it, perhaps even creating a new moment in your reality. This ability is the gift the South has given me, and with these images I repay it.

In a sense, work on *The American South* began at some indefinite point long ago when I first began to focus my education and experience through a camera. Work specifically done for the project, however, resulted from a year of travel through every State in the region during all four seasons. This travel, one of the grand experiences of my life, had the advantage of accelerating the image-making process and broadening the picture to interest those of us for whom place is an important element of life. More than that, the travel done for this book allowed me to create a portrait of a land and people as diverse as any nation's on earth.

Images of these travels have become a part of me. I remember a winter day, almost dusk, with sunlight slicing through a dry, polar air mass to burnish a forested Appalachian peak . . . a Saturday morning in Bardstown, Kentucky, with Main Street awakening in response to the rhythms that have governed American small towns for decades . . . night settling along U.S. 90, east of Marfa, Texas, and the infinity of the heavens descending, seeming to reduce the earth to the size of an asteroid . . . the rooftops of Charleston, South Carolina, marching in rows away from my viewpoint checkering the city below with color. Sometimes the experience was almost mystical; often it had the romance one might expect from a novel; rarely was it mundane.

As I traveled, I came to prefer the places that encompass both past and present. Mangum, Oklahoma, is fixed in my mind because of its dedication to local history. Small in size, lacking in any great wealth or long history, it nevertheless has a museum with a courtyard containing stone markers that offer brief biographies of every pioneer in Greer County. History as we define it is young there; the county was Indian Territory until 1907. But the people remember.

In Florida's Corkscrew Swamp, the National Audubon Society had the foresight to preserve some of the last remaining undisturbed natural area near the cacophony that is Naples-Fort Myers. In the stillness of a clear winter nightfall, I watched the swamp settle into silence, then was startled by an eruption of sound. A barred owl, sounding like some gigantic coyote, was staking its claim in the dusk. In its timelessness, Corkscrew Sanctuary offers an awareness of what south Florida once must have been.

And I revere the time spent with people who generously welcomed me into their homes and lives: Russell Guill, Sante Fe stationmaster in Canyon, Texas, for 30 years. Mr. and Mrs. Ross Sackett of Eureka Springs, Arkansas, for whom restoring fine Victorian houses has become a way of life. Shirley and George McCrary of Mooresville, Alabama, who found me photographing a Halloween display in their front yard and invited me in for much-needed food and conversation. Elmo Henderson of Blairs, Virginia, yard-sale bargain hunter without equal. R. L. Netterville, the Natchez attorney who introduced a stranger with a camera to the elegance of old Mississippi. And these are only a few.

Much of what seems important can be stated in one word: diversity. Understanding and preserving our diverse heritage, both cultural and natural, nurtures the potential inherent in our past and present. This, in turn, enriches and stabilizes life. There is little danger that America will ever become culturally bland and environmentally homogenized in its entirety, but in certain places and in some aspects of society it has already done so. The standardization of everything from education to subdivision design, even the modification of vast areas for single-crop agriculture, constantly pulls people toward the middle and tugs at an environment which must continue to sustain us both spiritually and physically. To the increasing multitudes who have never heard wild geese in migration, hiked the lonely ramparts of the Guadalupe Mountains, or seen Natchez or Charleston in the sweet fragrance of a warm spring night, these things do not exist. By preserving a broad spectrum of existence that includes them, we can prevent man from closing himself up and proving Blake true.

Industrialization bypassed the South for almost a century, and the region retains more than its share of cultural and natural diversity. Now that modernization has hit the Sunbelt fullblown, it is doubly important that we attend to its protection. Anything that brings awareness of our heritage in a genuine way, whether it be a book, a visit to a museum, or a wilderness journey, adds something to the potential for a richer future.

Though I traveled thousands of miles alone, I was never alone. The work of scholars, artists, preservationists, and all others to whom the expansion of human consciousness is central to life were with me. And if your awareness of the American South and its potential is expanded by this book, then you were with me too.

Boone, North Carolina
January, 1980

William A. Bake

Tobacco and Morning Fog. Valle Crucis, North Carolina.

xii

Foreword

To be attached to the subdivision, to love the
little platoon we belong to in society, is the
first principle (the germ, as it were) of
public affections. It is the first link by which
we proceed towards a love of our country,
and of mankind.

Edmund Burke
Reflections on the Revolution in France

Let me ask you, if I may, to come for a drive. It will not take long—55 years, more or less. Let us begin in Virginia, and begin again in Oklahoma, and then meander for a bit about the Deep South and the Carolina coast. In the dull stretches of highway, let us digress and reminisce, and think aloud about the South, but let us not get too profound about it all; and let us have periods of companionable silence to mark the flight of a heron in the Everglades or a blaze of autumn color in the Blue Ridge. Ours is a large area—fourteen States, 895,000 square miles of land and water—so we may fly now and then, if only for the pleasure of flying slowly into Lexington, Kentucky, on an April afternoon. Or we may sit quietly in a bateau in Louisiana, casting a popping bug toward a lily pad. We cannot see it all, not even in 55 years, more or less, but these have been among the travels of my lifetime. Come along.

We begin, if you will, in Virginia—more precisely, in Jamestown. Many years ago, when I first began coming to this quiet place, I ventured a word of advice. It is best to come here at dawn, before the tourists have descended, or at twilight, after the day's visitors have departed. Then the bricks and ivy of the ruined church tower whisper among themselves, and the foundation stones tell their own story in the silence. They speak in a proper English accent: *This is where it all began.*

To say it "all" began in Virginia is to engage in the kind of chauvinism that requires a narrowing definition. Elsewhere in the South, as eventually this land would be called, there had been French and Spanish expeditions before Christopher Newport's three ships came "up the King James, His River." And of course there had been Indians long before that.

The "all" that began at Jamestown was the first permanent English settlement in the New World. Each of us who lives in the South, and loves the South, has some particular place in the South that tugs most surely at the bell rope of memory. This is my place, here by the broad slow river, with grey gulls wheeling above the marshes and a cool mist blurring time and recollection. Ivy lies shadow-silent on the slopes that lead up from the shore. There are wild onions here, purple crowned, and a tangle of honeysuckle; and where the tide has gone out, leaving a wet spot behind, cloven tracks tell us that a deer has come this way. *This is how it must have been that spring and summer of 1607.*

Well, we tend to romanticize. We could not call ourselves Southerners if it were not so. It is an exercise in play-pretend to people the Jamestown stage with silver-buckled gentlemen in starched cuffs and shining swords. The playwright's directions are too tidy: at stage left, a stockade fence of pointed poles; stage right, a row of modest houses; behind a scrim, green fields and English gardens. John Smith is humming as Pocahontas enters . . .

No, it was not that way at all. Back in the spring of 1584, twenty-three years before Jamestown, Raleigh had led an expedition off Cape Hatteras. He had explored the largest island and called it Roanoke after an Indian word for wampum. Grenville had come this way. Virginia Dare and the lost colony had written their brief story. The "all" that began in Jamestown had its own beginning on December 30, 1606, when Newport launched his three ships into the New Year and the New World.

It must have been a wretched voyage. The *Susan Constant*, at 100 tons, was the largest of the three; her consorts were the *Godspeed*, 40 tons, and the tiny *Discovery*, 20 tons. (Three and a half centuries later, handsome reproductions of the ships would be built and tourists would marvel at how small the vessels were: all three could tie up on the wing of a Boeing 747.) Mid-February of 1607 passed before the cockleshell fleet could even get clear of England. On the way to the West Indies some of the crew attempted mutiny. It was not until May 6 that Newport took a landing party ashore at a point marking the entrance to a great bay. He wrote of "faire meaddowes and goodly tall Trees, with such Fresh-waters running through the woods, as I was almost ravished by the first sight thereof."

Newport was perhaps the first Southern romantic. He led his 104 settlers up the river 30 miles or so to "an extended plaine and spot of earth, which thrust out into the

Chicamacomico Coast Guard Station. OUTER BANKS, NORTH CAROLINA.

depth and middest of the channel." And here, in the midst of the meanest mosquitoes south of the New Jersey swamps, the "all" indeed began. By October, half of the band had died.

But it was in truth a beginning, and we remember it not in terms of a who and a when, as we remember Columbus, but in terms of a *place*. Jamestown was the first little platoon we belonged to in society; it was Burke's "first link" by which we would proceed to a love of our country, and of mankind. It was, as Newport said, a goodly spot of earth.

This is what this beautiful book is all about. William Bake set out many years ago to capture the essence of the South as a *place*. His first purpose was not to photograph people. That would be a fine enough purpose, but it was not *his* purpose. Through thousands of patient hours he sought the fields, the forests, the rivers, the mountains that both literally and metaphorically contain the roots of our inheritance. *This is our land*, and it is in truth a land for all seasons.

Are Southerners different from others in their fierce love of place? The idea may be, again, no more than a cherished heirloom in our attic of romance, but I think the tradition has substance. Virginians still honor John Taylor "of Caroline" and John Randolph "of Roanoke." Jefferson was the Sage of Monticello. The great plantations of the South, generation after generation, linked families to land. Jimmy Carter, before he became President, sought to identify himself to an interviewer. "I am a Southerner," he began, "an American, a farmer . . . " His expression of priorities sprang from the spontaneity of the moment, but it reached back a few centuries also.

William Bake's photographs speak of *place*, and they speak eloquently for themselves. My own assignment is to add these few words of evocation and description. I too am a Southerner, as my father was, and his father, and his father's father. My father's people were "the New Orleans branch." My mother's people had roots in Virginia and Kentucky. I myself was born in Oklahoma City, just twenty years into this century, at a time when Oklahoma City was as typically Southern as Baton Rouge or Memphis. I took my first newspaper job in Richmond, fell in love with Virginia, became an adopted son of the Old Dominion. My home is in the Blue Ridge Mountains of Rappahannock County. When I write of my land, my place, I write with Mr. Carter's priorities fixed in my own mind as firmly as Orion is fixed in the summer sky.

Parts of Virginia, I think, might be painted in pastels, parts of South Carolina in watercolor. An artist might try a green wash on the Gulf Coast, sepia on west Texas, pen and black ink on the coal towns of Kentucky. But a painter would paint the Oklahoma of my childhood in raw pigments, fresh from the tube. The Oklahoma skies of my recollection were rarely light blue, or dark blue, and never so fancy as "azure." They were just plain blue, as blue as the blue ribbon on the horn of a prize bull, and the landscapes stretched forever. The land was burnt orange and raw umber, and the rivers of my memory were as sandy brown as a brindle's back.

My mother's people, having long before put Kentucky and Virginia behind them, came down from Kansas. They were not "Sooners"—those were the few who came early into the Territory. They were '89ers, proudly identified with the Great Run. Their driving hunger was to hammer stakes in the hard red earth. I grew up with a school painting of the race that April day: dust in dirty cumulus clouds, horses open-mouthed, straining at traces taut on buckboards; and off to the side of this turbulent canvas, impassive Indians, expressionless, were looking on.

This was truly Indian country at the time of the run of 1889; it was less so when I was born in 1920, but the tribes left enduring marks behind. The cartography of Oklahoma remains a cartography of Comanche, Kiowa, Osage, and Pawnee. My father, a timberman, introduced me as a boy to the urban allures of Muskogee, Tahlequah, and Broken Arrow. We never thought much about the Indians. In school we learned something of the Five Civilized Tribes—the Cherokee, Chickasaw, Choctaw, Creek, and Seminole, each of them forming a nation entitled to hold its land "as long as grass shall grow and rivers run." I was a grown man before I realized how cruelly we had treated these Indian people in terms of their land, their place.

Some parts of Oklahoma have changed enormously since my nonage. Oklahoma City sprawls for miles; on those prairies a city finds abundant miles to sprawl in. Tulsa continues to look down its nose at its sister city. The story always was that the roughnecks of Oklahoma City drilled the wells and the tycoons of Tulsa sold the oil. Maybe that has changed a little too. But the wells still pump: mechanical anteaters, rhythmically rising and plunging, sucking black gold from red earth.

To remember Oklahoma is to remember those unhurried pumps and to remember derricks like steel saguaros on the skyline. By night the oil and gas fields were scenes from Dante: gas flares, billows of black smoke, figures in the gloom. In the Classen High School of my youth, dozens of classmates were tied by umbilical pipelines to oil. They were in the money or they were dead broke; boom or bust, there wasn't much in between. In my senior year one boy got an Auburn super-speedster for Christmas, a sporty job painted a lipstick red, with great chromium exhausts worming from the hood. It boasted a small brass plate on the dashboard: "This car has been driven at a speed of 101.24 miles per hour." That was at Christmas. By spring the Auburn was gone. So was my classmate. His father was a highrolling wildcatter whose roll ran out.

So it goes in oil. The story is told of an afternoon in October of 1957, when a group of editorial writers met in Oklahoma City. They went on a field trip as guests of an oil company. Mile after mile their buses rolled across a barren land. At last, out in the middle of nowhere, they gathered around a small fenced enclosure just as the sun was going down. Their host pointed to a concrete slab, neatly capped.

"We drilled a deep well here," he said. "It cost my company $1,403,527." He paused. "And the hole was dry."

That was the whole speech. The editors got back in their buses and rolled in silence mile after mile back to Oklahoma City. Not all economic education lies in textbooks. A man can learn something of venture capitalism and something of profit and loss out in the middle of nowhere.

I learned a few lessons myself about the nature of a marketplace economy—and about the limits of government—driving around Arkansas with my father. This would have been in the mid-thirties. He dealt in three main items: railway ties, fence posts, and bridge flooring. He drove a maroon Studebaker coupe in those days, and he drove it with a fierce concentration that brooked no backtalk from the car. Considering the Ozark roads we drove on, that was a good thing, too.

Several times we drove over to Fort Smith, on the Oklahoma line, and then explored Crawford and Franklin Counties in search of reliable sources of bois d'arc. That's pronounced bodark, incidentally. I think it's the same thing as the Osage orange. It made fine fence poles. A couple of times we went all the way to Little Rock and back by way of Hot Springs. Sulphur was thought to be good for you then. Every time father would see a stack of ties beside a railway track, he had to stop the car, walk over, and find out whether the ties were his or a competitor's. His brand was the Big K, with the K in a circle. We saw a lot of Arkansas that way—a beautiful and vastly underrated State.

The lessons in economics began to sink in around 1935 or 1936, toward the bottom of the depression. Farmers were too poor to buy fence posts; railways were picking up track, not laying it; and the highway people began to build bridges of poured concrete instead of 6 x 8 planks. The bottom dropped out, and father's business folded.

I said I also learned something about the limits of government. Father wasn't after bodark only; he was after corn liquor also. He used to bring it home from Arkansas by the case, in Mason jars. The Prohibition Amendment had been repealed nationally, but Oklahoma remained bone dry. In theory. Actually Oklahoma was as wet as the rain forests of Brazil. Oklahoma City must have had a thousand bootleggers. They advertised home delivery; they left calling cards; they provided charge accounts; and for years they maintained an unholy alliance with the Baptists to keep Oklahoma dry *de jure* and wet *de facto*. But father genuinely liked the Arkansas corn. He would stop by

Texas Bluebonnets. BANQUETE, TEXAS.

the Piggly-Wiggly and buy charcoal sticks, sold for just that purpose, and put one stick in every quart jar. It took the fusils out. After six months or so, the stuff was reportedly fit for strong men to drink. The government made feeble efforts to enforce the law, but this was a law that couldn't be enforced. Some things governments just can't do.

I said we were likely to digress. That was an Arkansas digression. Oklahoma and Texas learned all kinds of lessons in the thirties. We began to learn about land, how to conserve it by plowing on the contours. That was a lesson written in the dust on our window sills—dust the color of white pepper, finer than face powder, that seeped through the tightest windowpane. The wind never stopped blowing. Tornadoes and cyclones added to the misery. But most of the people hung on; they learned their lessons and they held their land. It was their *place*, their spot of windblown dusty earth.

And for all the Sunbelt surge of population in the sixties and seventies, it's remarkable how little has changed. Some of the huge ranches count their herds from helicopters and ride fences in Rovers, but cowhands never wholly disappear. Cattle still drift across the range as aimlessly as tumbleweed. The wheat fields are the same, a John Deere green in spring, toast brown at harvest time. Closer to the Southwest than to the Old South, Oklahoma and west Texas retain their restless vitality. We can drive forever in this country and still not get much of anywhere—but a distant hazy horizon always beckons, and the roads run straight as arrows.

We think of this part of the South, and usually we think of those wide-open spaces, the undulant fields, the barbed wire fences, the sheer incredible expanse of nothing at all. But the noise of the cities is as characteristic as the silence of the range. Dallas! Fort Worth! San Antonio! Houston! We punctuate their names with bang-marks.

In the autumn of 1979, traveling some of the same back roads that William Bake traveled before me, I drove from Houston east toward Birmingham and Charleston. If one major Texas city cries "Texas!" more vividly than any other, at least for me, it is Houston. San Antonio has one of the most colorful small riverfronts in the country; it is a city of red tiles and cool churches. Dallas is a Tiffany's window, glittering and rich. I think of Fort Worth: eggs and ketchup, white mugs of black steaming coffee, ten-gallon hats. Fine cities, these.

But Houston is all the Texas stories wrapped into one. Here you find the near-sighted millionaire. He hated to wear his glasses, so he had the windshield of his Cadillac ground to his prescription. And after going to all that trouble, why did he trade it in after six months? Answer: the ashtrays were full. Houston! Yes, parts of it may be as dull as Des Moines or as sober as Sioux Falls, but Houston is vigor unconfined. In the eyes of

Rising Mists. SHENANDOAH RIVER, WEST VIRGINIA.

a professional city planner, to be sure, Houston looks as if it fell off the back of a truck. Shopping centers bob up like meatballs in a freeway of spaghetti. You can drive thirty miles through Houston and never find a city; sometimes it seems there is no *there* there, but the impression is deceptive. Houston is the South's Chicago, one helluva town.

East of Houston on the road to Beaumont, power lines stretch to infinity. They are silver tendons on steel shoulders strung. This is a land of scrub trees, scrub cattle, scrub brush. The edges of the highway are littered with the black snake carcasses of blown-out tires. On the road to Baytown: phallic towers of huge refineries.

We stop at a service station for gas and directions. Two young Texans, booted and jeaned, are in total agreement—ain't but one way to go east, just follow I-10. I try to explain that we want to avoid the interstate and to go by less traveled routes. They are puzzled, incredulous. Who in Texas ever heard of going anywhere the slow way? Ain't but one way to Baton Rouge. We part on amiable terms, but a farewell rejoinder floats after me: Goin' to take you lots longer, mister. The signs in Texas say, Drive Friendly.

Twenty-six miles south of Beaumont lies Winnie, Texas, Pop. 1,543. That was its population in 1970, and it doesn't look as if the ensuing decade brought an explosion in the birthrate. Next to the Exxon station is a one-story red brick restaurant. Sign: No shirt, no shoes, no service. The menu lists one expensive delicacy: Cold Catfish, $7. (I pause long enough to voice indignation at the ignorant ridicule once heaped upon the Southern catfish. Fresh-caught in fresh water, the catfish is supreme among American piscatorial delights. If it were offered as Filet of Sole Alabama, gourmets throughout the land would fall upon it with cries of unaffected rapture.) Today I settle for the hamburger rare, then drive around the town. It doesn't take long, and the visit produces only one nugget of useful information: In Winnie, Texas, the super ice cream sundae is known as the Beltbuster.

This is flat land, flat and poor as a deuce of diamonds. There are several rivers—the Old River, Lost River, Trinity River—but of bird life very little. Cylindrical ammonium tanks, cone-topped, sit in little compounds: African villages of the new technology. Ahead of me a heavy truck blows a tire and drags itself off the road, a wounded animal pulling its foot from a trap. In a weed-grown field an old blue Ford, given up for junk, lies on its side like a dead bird. Poor country. But seventeen miles east of Winnie there is a directional sign: Country Club Road.

Port Arthur, now, and the towers of the refineries are as close as the masts of anchored schooners. Plumes of smoke add a panache to this spot of industrial earth. The Gulf waters today are the color of old rotogravure, but east on Route 82 the bayous are chrome blue. It is a landscape of dull browns and black birds, swamp grass, bony cattle, stores that sell bait and ice.

Bóvedas. TERLINGUA, TEXAS.

We idle into Louisiana, and the Gulf is off to the right beyond a rock-strewn, inhospitable beach. Farther out the offshore oil rigs can be seen, gaunt stalks with pistils served by helicopters big as bumblebees. Paint the houses softly—cream, pink, and yellow, and if it's a seascape you're doing, paint driftwood bleached as white as bones.

This is Cajun country, the name gently corrupted from Acadian country, and the French presence here is as tangible as the Indian presence in Oklahoma. It is pre-election time: Mouton for Governor, Gaspard for Clerk of Court, Reaux for Sheriff. In these parishes one shops at Dominique's Grocery, Hébert's Pharmacy, the Broussard Furniture Store. The regional delicacy is hot boudin, a French sausage seasoned to the asbestos tongues of the Cajun people.

The landscape slides by slowly: tiny homes, child's gardens, live oaks, a bayou clogged with hyacinths. There is a metaphor caught in those entangling growths. Until the mid-1950s, most of our people lived in a Southern bayou, clogged by prejudice and by tradition and moral blindness. An impenetrable mat had formed. The submerged mass had to be cut away, and we are the better for having the channel cleared. Some racism remains—you never can clean out hyacinths entirely—but our public waterways are freer than they used to be.

At Grand Chenier, we catch a first glimpse of Spanish moss. A venerable pecan tree, bending to the wind, is as bearded as John the Baptist. There's a metaphor here, too, if only I can get it straight. The moss is indigenous, an indestructible part of the Southern character; it blurs, conceals, softens, wraps the hard limbs of hard times in a fringed shawl. This is part of the Southern nature, to see through forests dimly, to bind the ugliest wounds in scraps of the finest petticoats.

It grows dark. We drive past fields of cane, and I search for a simile. Metaphors are hard going. The green stalks are as thick as—as what? Bristles on a paint brush? Matches in a pack? Passengers in a rush-hour subway? None of the similes works; it is late, and I am tired. At New Iberia a motel restaurant offers Cajun Fried Catfish. No Alaskan salmon ever tasted better.

In the morning, pushing on to Broussard and Lafayette, through plantation country, I see twists of ground fog, white scarfs for the live oaks. The two pump jockeys back at the Exxon station were right after all: there ain't but one way to get to Baton Rouge, on Interstate-10, yardstick straight for fifty miles across the swamps of the Atchafalaya River. This is fish country, duck country, alligator country; it is a land of rattailed possums, armadillos, wild pigs, muskrat, water spider, cottonmouth; green country, green as split-pea soup, and on a summer day it shimmers and sweats and swarms with insects. Now in October the lakes and bayous are as motionless as mirrors in an empty room.

The drive that runs on down to New Orleans provides time for aimless reflection. We digress. Eskimos have dog sleds, cowhands have ponies, New Yorkers live in taxis, and in parts of the upper Midwest no man seems ever to be far from his snowmobile. The Deep South has a different obsession: the pickup truck. Somewhere west of Abbeville I counted twenty oncoming vehicles in a row. Fourteen were pickup trucks. They are the ubiquitous beasts of all burdens, capable of carrying a cord of firewood, six coon hounds, and a dozen bags of feed. The pickup truck is the family sedan; it is the go-to-church limousine; it will take a man across a field to tend a calving cow by night. With a couple of rifles slung across the rear window, the truck is ready for a groundhog safari. It is stagecoach, buckboard, covered wagon, big mule. In these parts, stealing a man's pickup ranks with burning his barn or shooting his dog. A Southerner will cling to his pickup for years, until the front seat is rump sprung and the shocks have no more give than a baseball bat. You don't see many used pickup trucks advertised for sale. By the time an old Ford pickup gives up the ghost, there's not much use in it left.

For a second highway meditation: Another distinguishing characteristic of the South is the radio preacher. These rural divines hit the airwaves early in the morning, and they keep at it all day long. This is Bible thumping of the old school, holding tight to fundamentals, sinners facing the fires of hell. Repent! And while you're about it, brother, I'd thank you for five dollars so this work of mercy may be maintained.

Come to think of it, just coasting along through Ascension Parish, religion is extraordinarily important in the South. The Roman church still plays a major role in Louisiana and in the Spanish-speaking parts of Texas and Florida. In uppercrust Virginia the "Whiskypalians" exert a social and political influence out of proportion to their numbers. There are uppercrust Baptist churches too. Out on River Road in Richmond's fashionable West End, an elegant sign used to identify a handsome edifice: "River Road Church (Baptist)." The members were known around town as a new branch of the old faith. They were "Parenthetical Baptists."

Far more typical are the Baptists remembered by a gifted Southern writer, Maggie Ledford Lawson. She grew up in east Tennessee, right in the heart of the Bible Belt. There the winter revivals provided the principal religious and social events of the season. She tells of a typical revival at Cobbs Chapel, "just down the hollow from us, beyond the gap in Copper Ridge.

"Everybody comes—the saved and the unsaved, babes in arms, young girls hoping to find some boy to walk them home, neighbors who've not seen each other since early September. The truest believers sit on sideways benches at the front of the church. This is the amen corner, and there they function as a Greek chorus, commenting on the

action, the preaching, the praying, the shouting: 'Amen! God grant it!' Because almost no one in the congregation reads music, the church uses Stamps Baxter songbooks, with shaped notes, each note on the scale being represented by a different shape. After the singing leader sets the pitch, with a 'Do, Re, Mi, Do,' the faithful launch into 'Precious Memories.' After a long while comes salvation. Mourners come to a bench in front of the church, to be prayed upon and over. Sometimes a wayward sinner sits every night for two weeks upon the mourners' bench, but usually religious fervor does its work in a couple of hours, and the lost sheep, now filled with grace, rise up shouting to testify to the sanctification of being born again."

In such citified places as Raleigh, Atlanta, and Louisville, churches sometimes combine piety and gastronomy. Church suppers are a way of life. Louis D. Rubin, Jr., the Southern critic and historian, tells of a minister who spoke with modest complacency of a special feature of his urban "plant." He had "the largest barbecue pits south of Baltimore." Rubin mused that archaeologists from some distant planet, visiting the cindered Earth a few millennia hence, would marvel at the ruins: What bizarre religious rites, they might wonder, could have been served by these tremendous ovens?

New Orleans, now. On this particular trip I arrive in a tangle of midday traffic; the freeways are ordinary freeways; Canal Street might be Main Street, Anywhere. This is not the way to come to New Orleans. We ought to fly in from Lafayette in a small plane by night, when the river is a broad black ribbon of darkness and the streets of the city are necklaces of light. Just as Houston is a Southern Chicago, so New Orleans is the San Francisco of the South. Legends live here. Conventions come here. Odd characters dwell here. New Orleans is preeminently a port city, where the maritime logs in the morning *Times-Picayune* are studied as methodically as corn quotations are studied in the *Kansas City Star*. Ships come and go, flag-flowered; great trains of barges, like single column files of water spiders, crawl up and down the river.

But New Orleans is older than San Francisco; it is gentler; except in Carnival time, its pace is slower. In the drawing rooms of New Orleans, grandfather's portrait hangs in an oval frame. A dance card from some remembered Mardi Gras lies in an inlaid drawer. My own images are blurred by childhood's fuzzy focus on visits long ago; age has retouched them: worn red rugs, a sword in a tasseled scabbard, wine glasses that bell-chimed to a fingernail's flick, old silver serving dishes with sliding tops as round as a pigeon's breast. Streetcars were our cable cars: wicker seats with swivel backs, reversed at the end of the line in Audubon Park. Once I was taken to a cemetery, a silent city of small tombs with the porticoes of Greek temples, flights of alabaster angels. I think of New Orleans, and I think of taking my bride there soon after World War II. In a reckless

Mitchell's Handi-Market. FORT PAYNE, ALABAMA.

moment, I proposed to show off by drinking the black coffee of the French Market untouched by cream or milk. It was a short lesson in the drawbacks of bragging.

For the infrequent visitor, New Orleans probably remains forever fixed in memory as a city of masks and swirling skirts and doubloons flung from fairyland floats, a city of midnight jazz in smoky bistros, balconies as lacy as black negligees, honky-tonks, cheap beads, and tee-shirt souvenirs. The Quarter is all of that. But there is also the New Orleans of great oaks, big-limbed, where a boy could build a tree house as snug as a bird's nest; candles and murmurs and soft coughs of the first mass on a Sunday morning; and always, always, the river, the mud brown Mississippi, as deceptively tame as a pet lion, a force to be loved but never wholly to be trusted, the river that laps with soft little tongues at drowsy docks and then heaves its ugly weight upon the land in flood time.

This was my grandfather's place; I have the gold and silver spurs they gave him when he served as King of his Carnival krewe. It was my grandmother's place; she once was photographed, white-gowned, and at her throat a black velvet choker and a string of pearls. Such images are lamplit things, the fugitive shadows of an age I never knew. They carry echoes in a long hall of Chopin preludes poorly played; exercises for the left hand; the smell of creole gumbo, the cadence of black voices. New Orleans crowds the attic of the mind; it fills the chambers of the heart.

Heading east from New Orleans, a traveler crosses Lake Pontchartrain and sees the romance slide out through the rearview mirror. Once upon a time the area around Pass Christian boasted great summer homes, milk white mansions, tall-shuttered. Whole families descended late in May and stayed until mid-September. A boy could play croquet with his cousins, or if that seemed sissy stuff, a boy could walk barefooted across the road—the road that is now Route 90—and go crabbing by himself on the pier. On special occasions, when his father came out for the weekend, a boy might be taken fishing on one of the bayous off the Bay St. Louis, there to marvel at the shining iridescence of a croaker and the prehensile menace of a gar. After a boy of six—all by himself—has caught his first big largemouth bass, it is downhill all the way thereafter.

The mansions are gone now, gone with the hammocks and croquet wickets and the butterfly nets contrived of cheesecloth and coat hangers. Successive hurricanes swept the old gentility away and left a terminal moraine of ticky-tack behind. From Waveland east to Biloxi, the highway is one extended po' boy sandwich. The jewels of New Orleans yield to the glass rubies of stop lights, and the Gulf breeze carries not the warm scent of gumbo but the irresistible allure of a cheeseburger rare, with onions on the side.

Ticky-tack, I mean to say, is as much a part of the Southern *place* as the wild beauty of the Great Smokies. We tend to romanticize our land—cinnamon sachets in linen closets, sweet gardenias on the April air. Well, ours is also a land of sand in the sheets of summer cottages, and an eau de wet bathing suits on a screened-in porch. After Antoine's comes the Waffle House. The nearest Pizza Hut is never far away.

Let me harp on this theme for a moment. For a couple of hundred years it was part of our common parlance, growing out of the dark practice of human slavery, to speak and to write of *the* South. It provided a convenient shorthand distinction between the free States and the slaveholding States. With the War for Southern Independence, the dichotomy became fixed in our language; it was *the* South that seceded, and *the* South that ultimately surrendered; the Confederate States of America, a *de facto* nation, for four years held an accepted status of oneness. The image persisted through all the years of Reconstruction and into the Twentieth Century.

But except for the war years, there never has been any such thing as *the* South. There is not even a common speech. The accents of Memphis and Charleston are at least as different as the accents of Milan and Catania. Wildlife, birdlife, and plant life vary enormously across the region. Demographic analyses used to be written in terms of a black South and a white South, but there never has been any uniform pattern of racial distribution.

There is no such thing as *the* Southerner. We have elegant Southerners who ride to the Middleburg hounds, moneyed Southerners who lunch in the penthouse clubs of Atlanta, comfortable Southerners who ride their toy tractors around the lawns of Windsor Farms and Turtle Creek. We have black Southerners who still speak the Gullah speech of Summerville, and we have brown Southerners who speak the liquid speech of Spain. We have thousands of poor whites and more thousands of poor blacks who live at the poverty level. We have intellectual Southerners and illiterate Southerners, mountain men and oystermen, farmers, cowhands, deckhands, first violinists, and banjo pluckers. There is a pink coat South and a redneck South, a brandy-sipping South and a beer-swilling South. There is the hardhat South and the crinoline South, the earth-moving cane-cutting cotton-chopping apple-picking porch-sitting South. A child bride in east Tennessee may be stoking a kitchen stove at about the same hour a Charleston debutante comes home from a Christmas ball—Southern women, both of them, but women of wholly different Souths. William Bake's photographs speak of this immense diversity: not of one South, but of many.

Having said all that, let me add a few sentences more. Yes, I think there are certain characteristics that are sufficiently distinctive and sufficiently widespread that they may fairly be said to identify *the* South. Probably as a consequence of our climate, the pace of our life is indeed slower than the pace of life in San Francisco or Chicago. Our speech is slower, our public bodies more deliberate. Certain traditions—traditions of manners, traditions of style—remain embedded in a "Southern way." Among the first families of the South, the rule persists of *noblesse oblige*. D. Tennant Bryan, Chairman of the Board of the Richmond newspapers, once was given a civic award. The eulogist summed up his life in a telling phrase: "He always has done what was expected of him." The concepts of duty, and honor, and obligation are deeply held concepts in the South.

I don't want to assert flatly that the South, as a region, is more religious and more patriotic than other regions, but a good many years on the lecture circuit have taught me that one is more likely to hear grace before meals and the Pledge of Allegiance at a Southern luncheon than a Northern or Western one. I think Southerners, as a breed, are hawkier than others; the Citadel in Charleston and the Virginia Military Institute in Lexington have no counterparts anywhere, and they manifest the inheritance of arms. Until Vietnam, Southerners shared a unique distinction: Southerners were the only Americans ever to have experienced defeat. The legacy of 1865 has faded with the old flags, but down in Dixie many Southerners still leap to their feet at the first bar of their own rousing anthem.

I thought about all these things some months ago, driving back from Mobile through Pascagoula and D'Iberville to Gulfport: How different this Gulf Coast South is from my Blue Ridge Mountain South! From Gulfport I meandered through Hancock County, Mississippi, to Picayune, just to see if there *was* a town named Picayune. There was. Scrub pines, flat fields, at Carriere a rescue squad. Such squads are big community endeavors over most of the South—rescue squads and volunteer fire departments and church auxiliaries that continue to perform important functions of public welfare. This is the Deep South: total immersion in red-eye gravy. The land is home to some wealthy professionals and some prosperous merchants, but mostly it is home to po' whites and po' blacks, coexisting in their still largely separate worlds, jus' making do. It is farming country, but farming in a poor sense of the word. Farm ponds are set like Indian turquoise in the rolling bracelets of the meadows, but not many cattle come to use them. In much of the rural South families seep away. Between 1960 and 1970, forty-eight of Mississippi's eighty-two counties lost population. To an increasing degree, farm income here depends upon the forests. Row upon row, mile after mile, loblolly pines stand straight as schoolboys; they are growing up to be good pulp logs.

We have other institutions that bulk large in the South, among them high school sports. These also are taken seriously in the Midwest, I know, but down here they're a religion. I would not be surprised if a cultural historian, one of these years, discovered that America's only original art form, baton twirling, was born in the boondocks of

Winter Dusk; Bolivar Heights. SHENANDOAH VALLEY, WEST VIRGINIA.

Mississippi. If Southern high schools put as much emphasis on book learning as they put on marching bands, we'd have more youths who could spell and fewer whose talents got exhausted on the sousaphone. But let it go. At Poplarville the Hornets are playing on Friday night. Greenville has Hornets too. The Saturday morning papers abound with the feats of Panthers, Rebels, Bisons, Rockets, Trojans, Bulldogs, Wildcats, Warriors, Whippets, Raiders, and Tigers. The fledgling gridsters grow up to attend Auburn, Alabama, Ole Miss, Georgia Tech, and Tulane, and some of them spike touchdown balls in the Super Bowl.

Other sports are big in our country also—golf at Pinehurst and Augusta, deep sea fishing off the Florida Keys, stock car racing, quail hunting, sandlot ball. Southerners mow a million acres of grass on summer weekends, but that's exercise, not sport. Fraternal lodges are big in the South. At most of the colleges, Greek fraternities maintain Tudor mansions. Civic clubs proclaim their luncheons at every city limits. The smallest communities have bridge clubs, garden clubs, and ladies' sodalities. Southerners, by and large, are a gregarious people. Over most of the South, throughout most of the year, the weather provides no barrier to getting together. Southern hospitality is no myth; it's the real thing. There's an old story about the fifth-grader in a Christmas play in Charleston. In the role of the innkeeper he was supposed to answer Joseph's knock by turning him away. "No room! Go 'round to the manger!" Such rudeness was too much for a Southern boy. On performance night he improved upon the line: "I'm awful sorry. There really isn't any room in the inn—but come in and have a drink anyhow."

That was another digression. We were talking about Alabama, moseying along from Meridian to Birmingham. To tell the truth, it's not the most scenic country in the world. It's a blur of school buses, water towers, saw mills, shade trees, and country stores that bear an ensign as universal as the barber pole: Purina Chow. It's red clay country, the land clod-hard. I note cotton fields, small towns, a child's swing contrived from an old auto tire.

Birmingham has broad shoulders. It picks up iron and lays down steel, Pittsburgh of the South, a tough town. But the city has its soft edges also. Its growing medical center is a source of justifiable civic pride. There are libraries, colleges, concerts, lecture series, easy conversation in fine homes. Since U.S. Steel abandoned open hearth operations, the air quality has improved immensely—but something of the profitable soot of the old smokestacks has worked its way into the city's soul.

Montgomery, eighty-odd miles to the south, has a different character. Here was the capital of the Confederacy; here Jefferson Davis took his oath of office. It's a political town—I forgot to mention that politics is another indoor sport that's taken very seriously down here—and it has provided a legendary home for some of the most colorful characters in Southern political life. Up in Birmingham the smoke comes from steel; in Montgomery it comes from cigars.

Interesting thing about Alabama: You never think of Alabama in terms of water, except of course for Mobile, but if you swing north out of Birmingham to Gadsden, up to Huntsville, and back, you might be amazed at the lakes and ponds. The same is true of a drive south to Montgomery, east to Auburn and Opelika, and back over to Alexander City. There's a boat in every other backyard. You expect an abundance of lakes in east Tennessee, in the triangle formed by Knoxville, Nashville, and Chattanooga, but every time I fly over Alabama, or drive through it, I'm surprised all over again. This isn't upper Minnesota, by any manner of means, but in Alabama a man never has to go far to catch a fish.

If our conversation goes to matching cities, let me suggest that Atlanta is a kind of Cleveland of the South. The two cities are of a size; they're both sophisticated, wealthy, cosmopolitan, deeply involved in ethnic politics. But Atlanta excels in one particular: Atlanta has the most incredible airport in the world. It is incredible for this reason: Atlanta never stops building it. The Atlanta airport revives a medieval tradition: It took the Carolingians 300 years to build a cathedral. Atlantans may not lay their last brick as soon. Every traveler who flies around the South will have heard the standard joke: If you're flying to heaven, you'll have to change planes in Atlanta. There are other jokes: A fellow taxiing to the farthest Delta gate swears he peered through a rainswept window and saw a sign: Macon 24 miles. Another fellow tells me he once got a haircut in the Atlanta airport, set out for his gate, and had to have his hair cut again before he got there. That's a tall story, to be sure, but not very tall. Some city, some airport.

It's a long haul, clear across the state, from Atlanta to Savannah, but Savannah is a jewel of a city and not to be missed. Other old cities have done wonders in the name of urban renewal: Boston, Providence, Philadelphia, Baltimore, Richmond, Charleston. None that I know of has exceeded Savannah. It is a city to walk in, a city to live in. The whole of the center city is a sequence of squares, small in scale, comfortable as old sweaters, nothing pretentious. The antebellum townhouses that have gone to slums have been restored as private homes, law offices, boutiques, and book stores. And precisely because so many people live in the area and walk to work, Savannah is alive by day and night. There's not much glitter in Savannah—it's no little Atlanta and does not mean to be—but it provides a model of what vigorous community leadership can do in preserving values that ought to be preserved.

Savannah reminds me to make a point about this spot of earth we call the South: It is very much a spot of water too—salt water. Speak of the South, and word associations ordinarily link the South to land—to cottonfields, cane fields, tobacco barns, battlegrounds, Great Smoky Mountains. Southerners are also seafaring people. From Baltimore down the Bay to Norfolk, along the Atlantic Coast, around the Florida Keys, up and around the Gulf, all the way down to Brownsville, millions of Southerners attune their lives to the rhythm of surf and the music of wind in rigging.

North and south from Savannah lie the sea islands. They are moored to the land by lines of causeway, but their windows look to the endless sea. They are like Jamestown in this regard: They are best visited at dawn, after the waves have washed the beaches by night. Shore birds have done their needlework on the wet sand, stitching quick paths through seaweed and driftwood. The night's deposit of seashells awaits the solitary visitor. In *As You Like It*, the old duke found sermons in stones. He could have found sermons in seashells also. If you would be humbled by the infinite variety of God's designs and by the awesome perfection of the Jeweler's Hand, walk the beach at Hilton Head at sunrise and discover eons in a chambered shell.

We are drifting up the coast now to Beaufort—why it is pronounced Bewfort, only the natives know—and on to Charleston: palmettos, pines, faded gonfalons of Spanish moss, waterways as shallow as the lines on the palm of your hand, landscape and seascapes blending in blues and greens.

Images of Charleston spring to mind: great-grandmotherly houses, whose wide windows keep watch on children at play on the Battery; long piazzas, hung with ferns and flowering things; ceiling fans, old sideboards, she-crab soup, houses whose elbows touch like ten for dinner at a table meant for six. Tom Waring, for many years editor of the *News & Courier*, always spoke of Charleston as "the Holy City," an appellation accepted gravely by every true Charlestonian. The traveler who seeks the very essence of the Old South will find it at Middleton Garden, in lagoons of memory and forgetfulness, crushed blossoms of camellias, moss-hung paths that wind through thickets of azaleas to isolated glades. Here the clockhands stopped a century or so ago, locked in beauty and sadness cased in cameo. A red camellia shatters, shedding petal drops upon a spot of earth. An opal lizard, motionless amid the lichens, turns his jeweled head and looks with the ageless eyes of time past upon an intruder from time present.

North again, this time by the shore road through Georgetown and Myrtle Beach to Wilmington, North Carolina. An old friend has his small yacht there, and we go by the inland waterway on a luminous night in April. It is cool and clear and the wind is sharp; stars are caught in the pines like lights on Christmas trees. On such a night the highwayman came riding, when the moon was a ghostly galleon tossed upon cloudy seas, and the road was a ribbon of moonlight. We quote poetry and clap hands to keep warm; and an owl rises heavily from a dead cyprus to accept the applause with a bow.

Eventually we reach Portsmouth, and we are back in Virginia, hard by Hampton Roads and the Noble James. Up the river a few miles is Jamestown, point of beginning. There will be time, in other seasons, to speak of Florida, Tennessee, and Kentucky, to watch seeds grow and hillsides turn to tapestries, but it is William Bake's turn now. My images are transposed by the word, his by the camera's eye.

Spring

Spring climbs up the Southern latitudes like clematis up a trellis, one State at a time. It begins with the slow greening of fields in Alabama and an explosion of azaleas in South Carolina. It begins in Arkansas when the bass start biting. It begins in Oklahoma when cowhands move their cattle off wheat pasture. Over on the Atlantic Coast, it's spring when the master of a Maryland sailboat can take out his skipjack without wearing a sweater.

For the most part, spring enters gently upon the Southern stage, as shyly as a granddaughter coming into a room of grown-ups. It is a tentative entrance, accompanied by peeking and giggling, brief appearances, sudden vanishings. In Virginia, Kentucky, and North Carolina, the signs are deceptive. Early March brings a Monday warm enough and dry enough for plowing; on Tuesday it snows. On Wednesday the kitchen fire is blazing. On Thursday we fling open windows for the first time since September. Is it spring, or isn't it?

In the steep hills and hollows of east Tennessee, it's a different matter. Spring never comes gently in these mountains. Back in Virginia, on the genteel slopes of the Blue Ridge, a choreographer would put his dancers in tutus and bring them in on tiptoe to the shimmering strings of Debussy. Down in the Alleghenies, spring leaps on stage in a grand jeté, with all the horns of Sibelius fortissimo in the background. Cymbals crash and echo, kettledrums roll, and the wind and rain race wildly through the mountains. Freed from their ice captivity, rioting streams escape their banks. Bridges resist the flood, then surrender to it. Country roads lie axle-deep in mud. Underground waters blindly seek new channels; if you put your ear to a limestone rock, you may hear a river rushing somewhere in the Stygian darkness down below. The Appalachian farmer looks upon spring with stoic eyes: This too will pass, but there can't be any plowing till it does.

I spoke of mud and am minded to digress for a moment on Southern diversity. Our mud comes in all varieties. Elsewhere in the nation, dirt farmers have miles and miles of high-class dirt: The Iowa loam runs ten feet deep and stretches on forever; out in the San Fernando Valley of California, they tell me, the soil is so rich that a vegetable grower seeds at six in the morning and takes off a ton of celery by two. In parts of Florida and Texas, of course, they'd cut that celery by noon.

But much of our land is poor land. If many Southern fields were people, they'd qualify for food stamps. Too much tobacco, too much corn, too little rotation, too little topsoil to begin with. In the part of Virginia where I live, and in many parts of Georgia also, the soil is red clay; it doesn't crumble, it clods. Plowing this stuff, once it gets hard, is like plowing a brick sidewalk. The thaws of spring heave up the loosened stones of winter. Incidentally, a hundred years ago that was how slaves built the beautiful stone walls that bound so many fields: Men walked across a meadow like infantry platoons, tossing rocks in a bucket brigade toward the edges of the fields. When they were through, they had windrows of fieldstone waiting to be built into walls. Not that you can do much with them these days, but Rappahannock County rocks are an inexhaustible resource. It's getting rid of them that's exhausting.

Down in the Delta, some growers grapple with gumbo land; it never seems to dry out all the way. Parts of the Clinch Valley seem to have been fashioned from remnant scraps left over from the third day of creation—a few extra hills, some unneeded valleys, a thousand massive boulders that God discarded after God had made Vermont. Here you find a little of everything—red clay, blue shale, a streak of rich loam. A tobacco farmer, working a steep hillside in Tennessee, begins at the bottom in clay the color of peanut butter—the kind of clay that sticks to the soles of your feet. Farther up, the soil darkens into Dutch chocolate. Up another hundred feet, you may hit red shale that lies on the slope like shingles. When the torrents of spring wash over our graveled roads, what you have left is mud of a gooeyness unsurpassed in the nation. It's a distinction we'd as soon give up.

Floods and mud are among the hazards of spring. I haven't mentioned frost. From the citrus groves of Florida to the apple orchards of Virginia, frost is the enemy that knows no mercy. There is a critical moment in the formation of fruit. At such a moment a little frost can be tolerated; it can even be welcomed, for it does the work of thinning the buds. But a heavy frost that comes on a windless night leaves pure destruction in its ghostly wake. Fruit blossoms are prisoners on Death Row. They wait through anxious weeks for reprieve or execution.

These unpleasantries aside, spring in the American South can be as close to heaven as any of us will likely find on earth. Ours is the firmament that Marc Connelly wrote about in *Green Pastures*. Spring is best in the upper South, where the winters have been colder and the seasons are more sharply defined. Here spring awakes like a drowsy two-year-old, pushing aside crib blankets of snow. The first crocuses appear: tiny gold and purple jesters at the feet of regal oaks. The sun warms—for the first time in months it truly *warms*—and the earth yawns and stretches. We say, as we say of snow, that it *smells* like spring.

The stage fills. Imagine if you will—William Bake's photographs will help you— chorus lines of daffodils, turned out in cheerleader yellow. In our rock gardens, anemones advance upon April in ranks of toy soldiers. Confederate violets wave their flags. A moving paintbrush, working steadily up the hills, tints the countryside in green. On cue, the wildflowers enter—jack-in-the-pulpit, trillium, mayapples, bluebonnets, bluets, bouncing bet, trailing arbutus with leaves like leather slippers. The willows, hula-skirted, perform their own ballet.

In my own Virginia we wait for the dogwood. It is not easy to be patient with the dogwood. Weeks can pass while the buds, tight-jacketed, linger in the wings. We talk to them: What's the matter? We urge them, beg them, reason with them: Without the dogwoods, Virginia has no spring. And then, one April morning, they appear—cream white sails on a mint green sea, and suddenly our hillsides are alive. The dogwoods float in the forests as softly as clouds, the ivory blossoms tipped with brown; and by some marvelous stroke of color composition, they arrive in the company of redbuds. What costume designer could have done this? We drive along country lanes, not hurrying, taking our time, for when the dogwoods are in bloom every bend in the road enchants the eye.

The great attraction of spring, I am musing, lies in the change from stillness to motion. In our winters, at least in the Upper South, nothing much moves. Oh, we have windy days that fly smoke pennons from stone chimneys. When it snows, hay must be fetched to grazing cattle. There are ritual spurts of activity—hog killings, bird hunting, the logging of firewood. But hours pass when nothing happens.

With the first overtures of spring, it's a different matter. Southerners are inveterate gardeners. Flowers are a part of our lives to an extent not challenged elsewhere. The

New Moon at Breedlove's.
Oconee County, Georgia.

tiniest townhouses of Richmond and Charleston will have their flowered borders. Every high-rise apartment in Atlanta has at least a pot of petunias. Norfolk's azalea festival couldn't be copied in fireworks. We have rose gardens, herb gardens, camellia gardens, rock gardens, and gardens where day lilies lift their burnished copper trumpets. We have formal gardens, fashioned after those of Williamsburg; and we have informal gardens, fashioned after nothing at all. When the cherry blossoms bloom in May, Washington, D.C., is the loveliest capital in the world; Ladybird Johnson, with a little help from the Japanese, made it that way. Thanks to Mrs. Johnson, visitors can watch regiments of tulips in close-order drill. Mountain hillsides make their own gardens of laurel, rhododendron, wild iris. Trees play a part in this exuberant scheme of things—tulip poplars, magnolias, pink and white dogwoods. Arkansas' official state flower is the apple blossom, Florida's the orange blossom. What I am saying is that in this spot of earth we call the South, our gardens are glorious gifts of the gods, and we are grateful for them.

The spring that sets the gardeners in motion sets everything else in motion also. It is time to go fishing in the Carolinas, to go boating off the coasts, to watch the major leagues in their Florida camps, to try a new putter on the links of Hilton Head, or Jekyll Island, or Tarpon Springs. Southerners sometimes seem to be sports mad. And on the first Saturday of May, it's Derby Day in Louisville, bringing with it that remarkable rite of spring known as—the mint julep. Verily the day combines, as Kentuckians will tell you, the mead of gods with the sport of kings.

Everything moves—gardeners and golfers, daisies and dandelions, birds on the wing. The spaded earth reveals the wiggling worm, and the wiggling worm attracts a robin as big as a Canadian Mountie. The first purple martin scouts arrive in Virginia by the first of March. Bluebirds take up residence. Backyards are like the beginning of school: dormitories of finches, sororities of larks, a bustle of nest-building, food-shopping, girl-gossiping. The mirror ponds of winter shatter: Fish are rising, fish are spawning. It is not the voice of the turtle that is heard in our land, nor yet the voice of the power mower. It is the voice of the tiny tree frog at twilight, fiddling by the side of a swamp, that most surely signals the changing season. For months we have seen scarcely an animal. Now the warming earth releases chipmunks, rabbits, groundhogs, skunks. The snow silence of winter yields to an orchestra of busy sounds—mockingbird flutes, bumblebees on the bass viols. We are done with the largo movement in the symphony of seasons. In one great glissando: Spring!

Japanese Honeysuckle at the Lane. MIDDLETOWN VALLEY, MARYLAND.

The Home Place. CALDWELL COUNTY, NORTH CAROLINA.

Leanin' to the Plow. Blue Ridge Mountains, North Carolina.

Where He Was Young. MIDDLETOWN VALLEY, MARYLAND.

June Maples. TAMARACK, NORTH CAROLINA.

Odd Fellows Hall.
HARPERS FERRY, WEST VIRGINIA.

Indian Paintbrush. RICH MOUNTAIN, NORTH CAROLINA.

Jetstream Cirrus. Pickens County, South Carolina.

Potomac Passage.
Maryland Heights, Maryland.

Stonecrop on an Old Farm. WILSON COUNTY, TENNESSEE.

Coreopsis. LEBANON, TENNESSEE.

Skyline Dawn. SHENANDOAH NATIONAL PARK, VIRGINIA.

18

Hemlocks and Fog.
GREAT SMOKY MOUNTAINS NATIONAL PARK, TENNESSEE.

Overleaf:

Ship's Bones.
KIAWAH ISLAND, SOUTH CAROLINA.

19

Jackson Place, N.W. Washington, D.C.

22

At the Greene's. WATAUGA COUNTY, NORTH CAROLINA.

Queen Anne's Lace. HUNTSVILLE, ALABAMA.

The Sun Porch.
PASS CHRISTIAN, MISSISSIPPI.

Talking Over Old Times. SILVERSTONE, NORTH CAROLINA.

Savannah Saw Works. TELFAIR SQUARE, SAVANNAH, GEORGIA.

Bachelor's Buttons.
WATKINSVILLE, GEORGIA.

Antebellum Church.
MADISON, GEORGIA.

Rye and Lespedeza.
SCOTTSVILLE, KENTUCKY.

Mt. Dale S.S. Blue Ridge Mountains, North Carolina.

Patterns on Granite.
Stone Mountain, North Carolina.

Plainstyle Farmhouse and Camellias. Oconee County, Georgia.

Quiet Spring Evening.
Nolin River, Larue County, Kentucky.

Evening at the Conn-Meriwether House. MOBILE, ALABAMA.

The Pecan Grove. YUPON, ALABAMA.

Mirror Lake. BELLINGRATH GARDENS, ALABAMA.

Martha Tony.
MICCOSUKEE VILLAGE AND CULTURE CENTER, FLORIDA.

Winter Drought. EVERGLADES NATIONAL PARK, FLORIDA.

37

Nightfall on Menlo Street. FORT MYERS, FLORIDA.

Truck Gardens. HOMESTEAD, FLORIDA.

Atlantic Marsh at Dawn.
KIAWAH ISLAND, SOUTH CAROLINA.

Evening Along the Mississippi. NATCHEZ, MISSISSIPPI.

First Presbyterian Church (1859). PORT GIBSON, MISSISSIPPI.

42

The Ruins of Windsor. CLAIBORNE COUNTY, MISSISSIPPI.

Stanton Hall. NATCHEZ, MISSISSIPPI.

Keepin' to the Shade. PORT GIBSON, MISSISSIPPI.

To Satisfy A Southern Thirst.
BELLINGRATH GARDENS, ALABAMA.

Penny Scales. PORT GIBSON, MISSISSIPPI.

45

Cajun Country.
TAMMANY PARISH, LOUISIANA.

Ecclesiastes Prophesied.
LAFOURCHE PARISH, LOUISIANA.

The Rienzi Plantation.
THIBODAUX, LOUISIANA.

Jackson Square and the Cathedral of Saint Louis IX. NEW ORLEANS, LOUISIANA.

Evening Primroses on the Dunes. PADRE ISLAND NATIONAL SEASHORE, TEXAS.

Wavewash. PADRE ISLAND NATIONAL SEASHORE, TEXAS.

Wildflowers of the Hill Country.
LLANO, TEXAS.

Mission San Jose (1720).
SAN ANTONIO, TEXAS.

Imperial Barber Shop. Claude, Texas.

High Victorian. The Sidbury House, Corpus Christi, Texas.

Pasture's Edge.
KING RANCH, KINGSVILLE, TEXAS.

Gulf Surge. FISH PASS, MUSTANG ISLAND, TEXAS.

Summer

It is true of summer in the South, as it is true of just about everything about the South, that there isn't a single summer. There are many summers. They come in several sizes: good, bad, and crabgrass. Compared to an ordinary April in Kentucky or to a run-of-the-mill October in Virginia, the very best summer in Georgia is an inferior product. Ask a typical Southerner how he's doing, and the reply is likely to be, "Tol'ble, jus' tol'ble." That's the word for our summers: They are tolerable, just tolerable, but they are ours and we love them just the same.

Over most of the South, it is the heat, of course, that wears us down. Now and then, working in air-conditioned offices or driving in air-conditioned cars, we wonder how things were before air conditioning came along. If our curiosity were truly aroused, we could find the answer in any Texas tenant house, or in any patch of Alabama cotton, any day in July. In the late afternoon the sun hangs in the sky like a great fried egg on a blue steel griddle. Sensible folk find shade where they can, and down in the Deep South something akin to the Mexican siesta offers relief from the heat of the day.

I'm giving you the bad news first, wanting to maintain a reasonably impartial position on these matters. Summers in the South tend to be too much or too little. When we have too much sunshine and too little rain, the cotton wilts, the corn droops, and tobacco leaves close their eyes. Our country roads, muddy in the springtime, turn to burnt biscuits; you can tell a pickup truck is coming from a mile away by the rooster tail of dust it leaves behind. City streets burp little bubbles of asphalt. At such bases as Fort Bragg, Fort Benning, and Parris Island, troops learn Sahara lessons. They learn to maneuver in the bottom of a scorched kettle.

We also are afflicted, here and there, by too much rain and too little sunshine. When a Southern thunderstorm spits on its hands and goes to work, it provides an impressive exercise in violence. Thunderheads roll up, purple as bruises on the sky; the wind comes roaring with them; and rain lashes the land with fringed whips. Hail can add to the destructive misery. Radios are tuned for tornado watches. We won't talk about the hurricanes that hurl their terrifying power upon our coasts; we won't talk about them, we will only remember them.

After the slow waiting time of winter and the busy planting time of spring, summer is the growing time. By the end of May, tobacco plants are pushing at their canvas blankets, and the time has come to set them out. Early in the morning, preferably after a gentle rain the night before, the farmer brings his plants to the waiting plot in burlap sacks and lays them under some wet high weeds at the end of the field. On such a morning the air smells like freshly laundered linen on a country clothesline. Tree frogs are scurrying. There's a wisp of ground fog. A rabbit bolts from a fencerow, and a farm dog bolts after him. Husband, wife, and all the walking children share in the labor. One person pokes a hole in the moist earth with a sharp stick, wiggles it around, and the next person plops the plant in place and pats the earth around it. It's backbreaking work for the planter, but in a dry season it's worse: Then the holes have to be opened with a metal setter, and water has to be brought by bucket and barrel in a pickup truck. By the end of a day, half an acre is planted, though some of the feebler fellows will have to be reset later. The next morning sees the task resume. Let no one ever tell you that raising tobacco is an easy task.

Cotton is no cinch either. Or corn. Or soybeans. A part of the variety of the South lies in the variety of our natural pests. We have budworms, bollworms, earworms, cutworms, and army worms. We have Japanese beetles, sweat bees, and grasshoppers. We have fire ants, termites, snails, slugs, and white-faced hornets. The hornets are meaner than the yellow jackets and mud daubers. We have horseflies and flea beetles. I don't mean to be inclusive. If there's a bad bug, we have it.

We have rattlesnakes, cottonmouth moccasins, Gila monsters, and tarantulas as big as soccer balls. We have scorpions larger than lobsters. All of them come out in the summer. There are other pleasures. We have thistles with spikes as sharp as bayonets. We have crabgrass made of barbed wire. We have honeysuckle to choke the fences and water hyacinths to clog the bayous. We have quail that breakfast on our strawberries and groundhogs that lunch on ripening melons. Now and then our oysters are hit by the MX disease. There are times you can't swim in Virginia's tidal waters without having to dodge through a jellyfish quadrille.

I mean to be fair in these judgments, but I may follow in the steps of that legendary Savannah historian who published his masterwork a few years after The War. It was titled, so the story goes, "An Objective, Impartial, and Unbiased Account of the Late War for Southern Independence, Written from a Confederate Point of View." For all its drawbacks, a Southern summer is a marvelously pleasant season.

We have June nights that are as cool as the other side of the pillow, August evenings when the fireflies compete with shooting stars. Even the thunderstorms have a beauty all their own; they are cherry bombs and roman candles. When the growing season goes well, there's a tremendous satisfaction in our fields and vegetable gardens. On the farms we live by daily progress reports: Now the corn is tasseling, a jester's gavotte in the morning breeze. Today the tobacco is turning, the cotton squaring, the grapes ripening. In the barn the swallows return, presenting their flying circus; and soon the baby swallows peering over their mud nests view the audience in the fashion of black-tied musicians in an orchestra pit.

Summer on a Southern farm is mostly hard work. The longer the day, the more the hay; up before sun means more work done. Mechanization has eased some of the tougher chores. Many of our farmers—probably most of them—now use hay rollers instead of hay balers. These eliminate the exhausting business of heaving eighty-pound bales in and out of a truck. In the Delaware-Maryland-Virginia peninsula, poultry farming has progressed from an art to a laboratory science; from fuzzy chick to plucked broiler, production moves at stock car speed. But with all the technological improvements, most of our fruit still is picked by hand, and much of the labor remains: one man, one hoe.

There are compensations. In the heath balds around Asheville, old-timers know the delights of berrying. Early on a June morning, when the dew still glistens on rhododendron and laurel, you will find blueberries and huckleberries—I never have known the difference—that surpass all the store-bought berries ever sent to the supermarkets. Some wild strawberries linger on till June. In abandoned apple orchards, especially at higher elevations, you can pick merkles. They're also known as morels or *morilles*, if you like the French word, and they are the most marvelous mushrooms ever to spring up in shady spots. But merkles are rare, and their secret hiding places are passed down like dowries, a part of a farm wife's inheritance.

When the the Southerner is not working, he's loafing. This is different from waiting. Loafing is snoozing in a hammock; it is pole fishing from a moss-grown dock— and who really cares if a catfish has stolen the worm? In the cities it is porch-sitting or step-sitting. Some of us try to take off weight by watching the grass grow. When the moon is right, mill ponds invite the angler. Pond fishing is not nearly as strenuous as wading for trout in Rocky Mountain streams or killing salmon in Nova Scotia. That's *exercise*. The fellow who fishes for bass or bream takes his boat out before breakfast or after an early dinner. He uses a fly rod so light you could mail it for 15 cents. His lure is often a popping bug. The idea is to cast the bug so that it lands lightly upon the placid water, as softly as a real bug falling off an overhanging limb. The bug twitches, struggles, flounders. *Wham*! A big bass, silver-armored, takes the gauntlet and runs for safety in lily pads or in the submerged tops of fallen trees. Sometimes he's home free; sometimes he's Sunday morning breakfast. Even when the fish refuse the most artistic cast in the most inviting water, pond fishing remains the most Southern of Southern pastimes. It is slow; it is easygoing, undemanding, contemplative; it does not require a foursome, as in golf, or even a partner, as in tennis. I know a millpond in King William County, Virginia, a part of the great plantation known as Elsing Green, where a man scarcely needs to cast his line at all. The fish, on command, obligingly leap into the boat. Or if actually catching fish is no particular object, an angler can simply drift along in his skiff, alone, while tensions drip away like water off a paddle.

There are more gregarious ways to get away from work. Baseball is no longer the obsession that it used to be, but it still reigns supreme among the Southern sports of summer. The South once was baseball crazy. The Texas League was founded in 1888, the Southern Association in 1901, and the old Sally League—more formally known as the South Atlantic League—in 1903. Ty Cobb came out of the Augusta team in the Sally. He may have been the greatest all-around player in the history of the game.

Once there were so many leagues—the Southwestern, East Texas, Rio Grande Valley, Alabama State, Tobacco State, Virginia, Gulf Coast, Florida International, Piedmont, Cotton States, Evangeline. *Eheu*! It is mostly a roll call of the dead. In 1979, Atlanta, Houston, and Dallas-Fort Worth fielded teams in the major leagues; only Richmond and Oklahoma City fielded Triple-A teams in the minors. But two Double-A leagues survive in the South—the Texas League and the Southern League—and a bit lower in the hierarchy one finds the Carolina, Florida State, and Western Carolina Leagues. There's a Gulf Coast League for rookies. The old obsession still lives in a thousand sandlot aggregations and in slowpitch softball clubs. A part of the charm of baseball, as Eugene McCarthy has written, is that time plays no part in the rules; in theory, a game could go on forever, inning after endless inning, the score always tied. Believe me, a game in which time doesn't matter is a game that Southerners will never abandon.

So our summers pass, working and loafing, and the mountains are somnolent and the swamps are drowsy. The days wash away like castles of sand, and August ends too soon.

A Successful Garden. COLONIAL WILLIAMSBURG, VIRGINIA.

Maryland Heights.
HARPERS FERRY NATIONAL HISTORICAL PARK, MARYLAND, WEST VIRGINIA.

H.F. Berly. Amherst, Virginia.

Nicholson Street, Evening. Colonial Williamsburg, Virginia.

Along the Old Road. LOVINGSTON, VIRGINIA.

Charolais in the Shenandoah Valley.
SHEPHERDSTOWN, WEST VIRGINIA.

Shattered Oak. WINSOME MOUNTAIN, NORTH CAROLINA.

Johnboat at Dawn.
SHENANDOAH RIVER, WEST VIRGINIA.

Along the West Ridge.
Tangier Island, Virginia.

Six Days Shall Man Toil. TANGIER ISLAND, VIRGINIA.

Crab Pots. TANGIER ISLAND, VIRGINIA.

August Evening. TANGIER ISLAND, VIRGINIA.

The Irene and Pearl II. TANGIER ISLAND, VIRGINIA.

Rose Mallows and Morning Mists.
CHINCOTEAGUE ISLAND, VIRGINIA.

White Bear Ridge.
Wind Prairie Preserve,
North Carolina.

78

Last Muster at Antietam.
SHARPSBURG, MARYLAND.

79

Greer Ranch. SPRUCE HIGH COUNTRY, NORTH CAROLINA.

Hemlocks on the Rim. LINVILLE GORGE WILDERNESS, NORTH CAROLINA.

Big Meadows.
SHENANDOAH NATIONAL PARK, VIRGINIA.

Shelf Fungi. THURMONT, MARYLAND.

83

Rain in the Air. MAYSVILLE, GEORGIA.

Church of God. WHITE COUNTY, GEORGIA.

Cloudfront and Evening Light.
WINDBLASTER DIVIDE, NORTH CAROLINA.

85

Piedmont Elegy. APALACHEE, GEORGIA.

Toward Whitehall. OCONEE COUNTY, GEORGIA.

87

Winebarger Mill, Early September. MEAT CAMP, NORTH CAROLINA.

First Touch of Autumn.
WINSOME MOUNTAIN, NORTH CAROLINA.

Fragrance on a Fenceline.
HODGENVILLE, KENTUCKY.

Out of the Fog. WATAUGA COUNTY, NORTH CAROLINA.

Appalachian Pastorale.
SMOOTH SHOULDER RIDGE, TENNESSEE.

Survivors. WILSON COUNTY, TENNESSEE.

92

Last Car Home. NASHVILLE, TENNESSEE.

Fair Time. BAIRD'S MILL, TENNESSEE.

The Centre Family Dwelling House. SHAKERTOWN AT PLEASANT HILL, KENTUCKY.

Morning Pastures. SHAKERTOWN AT PLEASANT HILL, KENTUCKY.

Mainstreet at Midmorning. HARRODSBURG, KENTUCKY.

Julian Taylor. SPRINGFIELD, KENTUCKY.

Autumn

How do we grade our autumns in the South? Like wine, I think, for in the mountains I know best—the mountains of Maryland, Virginia, and North Carolina—our autumns come in vintage years. All of our Octobers are drinkable, but some Octobers are like some Burgundies. They glow with an inner fire. Such autumns are meant to be sipped—amontillado autumns, if you please, when the oaks are as tawny as sherry. Such autumns ought never to be hurried.

It needs to be said again, as we say of other seasons, that the South has half a dozen autumns. Down in the Deep South, seasons are old soldiers; they tend to fade away. Green pastures slowly go to seed in August; gardens tail off; gradually our lawns turn as tan as field mice. There's nothing very spectacular here. Autumn in most of Alabama, Mississippi, and Louisiana is merely a time that is cooler than summer and not as cool as winter, and if it weren't for certain festive occasions and for high school and college football, November might as well be March.

We tend to forget the mountainous South—the Ozarks, Appalachians, Alleghenies,

Great Smokies, Blue Ridge, Catoctins. In the higher elevations around Boone, North Carolina, where William Bake lives, autumn can be pure pageantry. This is how October must have been in Camelot—bronze shields and silver lances, flags and pennants, all the old heraldic emblems, red lions of maple rampant on a field of poplar gold. Dreaming away an upland afternoon, we people the wooded hills with armored knights, ladies-in-waiting, monks in brown cassocks, Scottish lords in swirling kilts. The imagination supplies priests, bishops, cardinals robed in redbud, harlequin persimmons with turned up toes. To walk in these woods in autumn is to walk in God's own cathedral—a Gothic tracery of arches, columns, vaults, and buttresses, with the sun striking dusty shafts through stained glass windows. Images crowd the mind, of tapestries and Oriental rugs, of locust leaves as mottled and veined as the hands of old men. Mountain people often are poor people, but they own jewels and precious stones in fall—emerald pines and topaz hickories, fire opals in a hedgerow, aster sapphires by the road.

Under the spell of such an autumn, the Southern tempo quickens. No time for loafing now! These are the days of harvest, when cotton moves to the gins and combines growl their way through fields of soybeans and corn. Growers are picking tangerines in Texas, apples in Virginia, and down around Fort Myers, Florida, they're cutting pompons and chrysanthemums. Peanuts move to market. So do pecans. And in many a country kitchen, the flat iron that sits on the back eye of the stove gets put to a ritual use: It's the finest tool ever invented for cracking black walnuts.

In the Carolinas, Kentucky, Tennessee, and Virginia, all the labor of the tobacco grower comes at last to fruition. The times vary according to the variety of tobacco being grown and the kind of cure required; auctions run from late summer to well after Christmas. Throughout the growing season, in an effort to keep the plants from getting leggy, farmers have been breaking off suckers and cutting the pink and white blossoms that form at the top of the plants. The closer the ground, the better the leaves. Little by little the plants turn from green gold to old gold, and by late August or early September the burley is ready for cutting. Men move up and down the head-high rows, cutting tobacco leaf by leaf, each leaf as large as the blade of a ceiling fan. The leaves are skewered upon spears and then taken to barns to cure in September's easy air. (Flue-cured tobacco, of course, involves a different process and some quite intoxicating scents, but it's basically all the same.)

When auction time rolls around, the burley grower prays for a damp, penetrating cold—the kind of cold that gets under the skin like a splinter. On such days the tobacco comes in case, meaning the leaves are pliable, or literally fit to be tied. On a couple of long boards set on sawhorses in the barn, the grower carefully separates the cured tobacco into the valuable cutters and ground leaves in one pile, and the less valuable long reds, short reds and tips in another. After further sorting and grading, two or three farm wives then tie the tobacco into "hands." The finished hands, looking like turbaned dolls, are piled into baskets. It's finger-numbing work, but there's always a warm fire not far from the barn, and often the labor is eased by hot biscuits filled with peach butter and bits of tenderloin fried to a golden brown.

A tobacco auction combines some of the elements of a county fair, a precinct picnic, and a Latin mass. In the mountains of Kentucky and Tennessee, many families still get to town infrequently. Their big trips come in spring, to buy seed and fertilizer, and again in the late fall or early winter to put their baskets of tobacco on a warehouse floor. The fall trip provides the festive occasion. An auctioneer moves swiftly down the windrows of fortune, performing his gobble-gobble litany as buyers from the tobacco companies signal their bids. It's all over in an hour or two. With cash money in their pockets, farmers head for Main Street and the colored lights of Christmas.

Autumn brings other occasions for the get-togethers that lighten the tedium of country living. In the Blue Ridge Mountains, after the apple harvest is over, three or four families combine their resources to make apple butter. It's an all-day process, starting at sunup with the peeling and coring of windfalls. The men have built a backyard fire and positioned an enormous iron kettle to cook the apples down. The mixture of apples and spicy seasoning has to be stirred constantly with paddles, and quart jars have to be sterilized by the time the butter reaches its perfect consistency. The end product has a sweet tartness or a tart sweetness—take your choice—and it lifts cornbread or bacon biscuits to Olympian levels.

The making of country sorghum follows the same procedure. You pick an evening in October, when the air is crisp as apples and a pumpkin moon is out, and you leave word at the country store that a stir-off will be held. Fifteen or twenty neighbors gather— old men and maiden aunts, young couples with lap babies, farm boys in hand-me-down overalls. The older children sit about on logs, sucking sweet juice from stalks of raw cane, sometimes cutting their tongues in the process; the teenagers fetch logs to keep the fire just right; and gradually the cane cooks down to green and gold. It's midnight before the sorghum gets ladled into fruit jars. It will last the winter long.

Come to think of it, such festive occasions probably are the making of our autumns. Every Southern State has its State fair, and there are hundreds of county fairs as well. Perhaps city youngsters have the equivalent of the Four-H and the Future Farmers of America. I wouldn't know. But for high excitement, let me nominate the kind of competition among 14-year-olds that produces a blue-ribbon heifer, a prize steer, or a sheep with imperial airs. Here the sawdust tents are crowded with long tables of pickles, relishes, jellies, ears of golden corn, cakes to be sold for the ladies' auxiliary. Over on the midway a calliope is sawing the autumn air. County fairs smell of popcorn, cotton candy, and grilled hamburgers at the booth of the Rescue Squad; and if you're hanging around the livestock exhibition, county fairs smell of something else. They're institutions, these fairs, as much fun as they were in the days of Chaucer.

I've mentioned football before. The game is played with passionate partisanship at both the high school and the college levels. On the Saturdays that Oklahoma meets Texas, or Alabama tangles with Ole Miss, it is said that the crunch of opposing lines on the opening play can be heard for fifty miles. The roar of opposing alumni can be heard a bit farther on.

Autumn is revival time in many a Bible Belt church. With crops harvested and the children back in school, there's a breathing space to pump up the old-time religion. Some years ago the *Richmond News Leader* had a venerable religion editor by the name of Robert Beverly Munford; he was a portly old gentleman, his pink face haloed in white hair. As the revival notices streamed across his desk he was heard to complain petulantly that "the faith of these people must be very weak—very weak indeed, sir, very feeble— for it has to be *revived* all the time." Whatever the explanation, the churches undergo a remarkable surge of activity. I happened to be in Memphis one October when the *Commercial Appeal* carried a notice in its Church Calendar: "The Jesus Explosion will present a Christian Fashion Extravaganza at 4 p.m. at the Sarah Brown Branch, YWCA." That same week a Texas evangelist, visiting in Shelby County, was conducting a three-night, six-hour "walk" through the Bible from Genesis to Revelation, "using 1,000 graphic and visuals projected on a screen, including transparencies, color slides and cartoons." Down in the Delta country, as Walter Cronkite might say, this is the way it is.

Throughout the South, autumn means hunting. In the coastal marshes of Virginia and the Carolinas, men seek the elusive sora. Over most of the area we have quail. In a few mountainous counties the skilled hunter can flush pheasant and grouse. Following their ancient migratory paths, ducks and geese stream across our skies. Doves hang around for much of the year. On opening day of the deer season, many a rural Southern county simply closes its public schools: Not enough farm boys would show up in class to make the effort worthwhile. For them, getting a deer can mean a hundred pounds of meat for the winter. Nobody takes deer hunting lightly.

In some areas, October means 'coon hunting or fox hunting. They're related in about the same way that Burger King is related to Le Papillon. Fox hunting demands, for starters, a fox, a pack of hounds, a master, a couple of whippers-in, pink coats, proper dress, stirrup cups at cast-off, and a hunt breakfast at the end. And of course the sport requires a field of men and women with a consuming urge to risk their precious necks over rough brush and stone walls. The riders kill very few foxes, but they break a good many bones. 'Coon hunting is night hunting, when two or three old-timers take half a dozen red bone, blue tick, or black-and-tan hounds out for an evening concert. The terrain has to be moist, but not too moist; any excess moisture is contained in a little brown jug. Critics tend to divide on the quality of the entertainment. Veteran night hunters hear the cry of their hounds as the sweetest music this side of the heavenly choirs; you get that point of view in "The Voice of Bugle Ann." For the dedicated 'coon man, his hounds are the trumpets of Purcell and the horns of Wagner, bugles of brass and cornets of silver. But there are those, alas, especially on the fourth sleepless night in a row, who are reminded of the yowl that is heard when a heavy-footed fellow trods on the tails of a tomcat convention. It's all a matter of musical taste.

Have I left anything out? I haven't touched upon our Thanksgiving dinners, the first of which was held at Jamestown in 1607, long before the Pilgrims took the arrows out of their hats in Massachusetts. A typical Thanksgiving dinner, almost anywhere below the Mason-Dixon line, might begin at high noon with peanut soup, continue through oyster stew, spoonbread, cornbread, beaten biscuits, Brunswick stew, turkey with walnut dressing, Smithfield ham, Carolina ham, Georgia ham, Kentucky ham, crab gumbo, broiled quail, candied yams, and assorted vegetables—and wind up two days later with peach cobbler, apple pie, and Alka Seltzer. Southerners do dearly love to eat.

And they love their land. With deference to the other seasons, and especially to spring in Albemarle County, Virginia, autumn is the best we have. The fall brings our people together in State fairs, county fairs, football games, church revivals, hog killings, and sorghum stir-offs. Autumn turns much of our land to Persian rugs and patchwork quilts; and seen from the wing of a falcon or the eye of a catfish—or through the lens of William Bake's camera—our spot of earth may modestly be described in autumn as the loveliest spot of all.

Autumn Haze. GRAYSON COUNTY, VIRGINIA.

104

Laurel Creek.
GREAT SMOKY MOUNTAINS
NATIONAL PARK, TENNESSEE.

Shadows on the Potomac. LOUDOUN HEIGHTS, VIRGINIA.

Boxelders Along the Shenandoah. HARPERS FERRY, WEST VIRGINIA.

Wolf River Apples. TROUTDALE, VIRGINIA.

Fir in Mountain Oatgrass.
ROUND BALD, TENNESSEE.

108

Harvest Veteran.
MEAT CAMP, NORTH CAROLINA.

Waiting For Nightfall.
VILAS, NORTH CAROLINA.

The Store Room. WATAUGA COUNTY, NORTH CAROLINA.

Harper's Window. HARPERS FERRY NATIONAL HISTORICAL PARK, WEST VIRGINIA.

112

Zittlestown. Washington County, Maryland.

Linville Creek Road. Vilas, North Carolina.

Price Lake; Indian Summer. BLUE RIDGE PARKWAY, NORTH CAROLINA.

Country Garden. TODD, NORTH CAROLINA.

117

Burley. Mountain City, Tennessee.

Late September.
Valle Crucis, North Carolina.

Dry Pump. JASPER, ARKANSAS.

Leaf Fall. BOONE, NORTH CAROLINA.

Maples on Lincoln Road.
ROUND HILL, VIRGINIA.

New River Farmhouse.
ASHE COUNTY, NORTH CAROLINA.

Rain on the Broomsedge. MURPHY, NORTH CAROLINA.

Saturday Morning at Meat Camp.
WATAUGA COUNTY, NORTH CAROLINA.

Requiem for Autumn. RICH MOUNTAIN, NORTH CAROLINA.

"Confederate Daisies" (Viguiera porteri). STONE MOUNTAIN, GEORGIA.

Piney Woods Autumn. LAKE GUNTERSVILLE STATE PARK, ALABAMA.

Goldenrod. WHITE COUNTY, GEORGIA.

The McCrae House. WATKINSVILLE, GEORGIA.

Autumn Market. FORT PAYNE, ALABAMA.

129

Cotton Was King. Bishop, Georgia.

October Interlude. Mooresville, Alabama.

Beeches Along the Buffalo.
BUFFALO NATIONAL RIVER, ARKANSAS.

Under Autumn Skies. DEKALB COUNTY, ALABAMA.

134

Leaf Raking Time. FORT PAYNE, ALABAMA.

The Little River. GREAT SMOKY MOUNTAINS NATIONAL PARK, TENNESSEE.

Ozark Pasturelands.
MADISON COUNTY, ARKANSAS.

Kingston Mercantile.
KINGSTON, ARKANSAS.

Bunch's Store (detail).
KINGSTON, ARKANSAS.

Pearl's Cafe.
JASPER, ARKANSAS.

Sackett's Porch. EUREKA SPRINGS, ARKANSAS.

Spring Street. EUREKA SPRINGS, ARKANSAS.

141

Winter

Winter in the Deep South is one thing. Winter in the Upper South is something else. The big difference is that winter in the Deep South offers a time and place you'd like to go to, and winter in the Upper South produces a season you'd often like to get away from.

Speak of winter, and the mind conjures a vision of drifting snow, penetrating cold, old buildings with icicle beards. No one thinks of the South in those terms. Our land, after all, is universally known as the "Sunny South." To the songwriter, the sun really shines all the time—and if you're fishing for marlin off the deep blue waters of Key Largo, this is all very true.

Deep in Dixie, winter has its charms. By the first of December the tourists are streaming to Miami and Orlando. They home on Jacksonville and Lauderdale like migratory ducks, and they seek the sun as hungrily as houseplants reaching for a Southern window. Until early March they fill the Florida bus stops: flocks of black and yellow grosbeaks on an asphalt limb.

From Tampa around the Gulf Coast to Corpus Christi, the winter season is the busy season. New Orleans opens its arms to the revelers who come for Mardi Gras. In the Rio Grande Valley, it is shipping time for oranges and grapefruit, planting time for cabbage, cauliflower, cucumbers, and tomatoes. Now and then, to be sure, the winter months remember that they are expected to be winter months. Birmingham can post a high of 75 on one day, of 22 the next. The Oklahoma Panhandle can match its blizzards with the best of those that hit Nebraska. In northern Louisiana and Mississippi, January can bring any kind of winter that's listed on a menu. But for the most part, winter in the Deep South means warm sand and hot days, sunglasses and suntan oil, whitecaps on blue water, and a long cool drink in the late afternoon.

Tell it not to the envious mountain families of eastern Tennessee and Kentucky, to cowhands in western Oklahoma, or to oyster tongers whose hard living is wrung from the freezing waters of Chesapeake Bay. They sell no suntan oil in Sperryville, Virginia. Mind you, I am not suggesting that our Virginia snows rank with the blizzards of Colorado; our snows are more genteel; they knock before entering the county, and they seldom stay for long. For the most part these are well-mannered snows, not so rude as the snows of Chicago or as overpowering as the snows of Buffalo. But they can chill the very bones.

Winter is our waiting time. In the Blue Ridge Mountains, clocks go into hibernation in November and tick slowly in the silence unto March. The same sense of suspended animation pervades the mountain country farther south, in the Alleghenies and the Smokies. The somnolence affects farmers in Kentucky and Arkansas, ranchers in the Marlboro country around Amarillo. Every week seems a slow motion replay of the week before. And we do indeed get snow.

It cannot be mere imagination—there must be some physical explanation for it—but our snows signal their coming in perceptible ways. "It smells like snow," we say, and the smell is as palpable as the smell of simmering sorghum. "It looks like snow," and the sky fills with the grey cotton wipe towels that mechanics use. Before the first snowflake appears, bird feeders swarm with lunch hour crowds. On the hillsides, sheep and cattle find upwind shelter.

When the snow comes, it may come a foot at a time—nothing at all, I repeat, for the frostbitten folk of Great Falls, Montana, but in the Blue Ridge this is snow of arctic dimensions. Our hilly upland pastures turn to mountains of whipped cream, windswirled. Split-rail fences form a rickrack hem around white-sheeted meadows. The most lordly pines sag under the weight of ermine capes. And in the silence that follows a snowfall, nothing moves.

It is a scary thing to be literally snowbound in our mountains. The imagination takes flight with the sparrows: What of a fire? What of a broken bone? What if a baby decides to be born? Emergency equipment could never get through. When the electric power goes out, the cozy romance of being snowbound loses its appeal; lanterns will do for light bulbs, and wood stoves may keep us warm, but once the water pump quits, country living has no charm.

There are compensations. Samuel Johnson, who all his life hated to be alone, once remarked to Mrs. Aston that "solitude excludes pleasures, and does not always secure peace." He was only half right. There are indeed great pleasures in solitude, some of them negative pleasures—the pleasure of not being able to pull stumps, the pleasure of not having to tolerate the uninvited guest. There are positive pleasures also in a snowbound time—the reading of books too long postponed, the catching up on little things around the house. And there always is the comfortable certainty that after a while—much too soon—the highway department will send its snow plows, great orange beetles with iron foreheads, and open the roads again.

In the waiting time we read the seed catalogues. How on earth, I have wondered, did farm families a hundred years ago survive their winters without them? These exercises in four-color optimism begin arriving well before Christmas; they pile up ten deep in a grandchild's high chair. Such catalogues are meant to be sipped and savored; they are meant to be weighed like wines against one another; on the one hand, Park; but, ah, on the other hand, Burpee. On the coldest afternoons of winter, we thus hold in our hands a hybrid Big Boy, red as hickory embers, big as a softball, warmed by the sun of August. The kitchen fire flames with an imaginary harvest—yellow squash, golden corn, scarlet peppers. We fly from February's prison on the dreams of next July.

There is of course much work to be done, even in the waiting time. Long before wood stoves became city-fashionable, as a kind of poverty chic, rural families depended heavily upon their woodlots. Firewood has to be cut; it has to be stacked and seasoned; it has to be brought to the house; and once burned, the ashes have to be dusted on the compost heap or floured on a patch of asparagus. Tools have to be repaired, harness refitted, stalls painted, tax forms prepared. Along the coast there are nets to be mended, boats to be tended. Work never wholly stops.

If you're into tobacco, work never stops at all. In Hawkins County at the tip of eastern Tennessee, tobacco beds must be put in order. On a bleak day in January, when a pale sun provides an illusion of warmth, cedar brush is spread over the plot—a spot of earth maybe five furrows wide and thirty feet long. The pyre is set afire to burn out the weeds. It smolders for two or three days. Then store-bought fertilizer and homemade manure must be raked into the bed, the tiny black seeds planted, the plot cribbed with logs, and the whole blanketed with flat canvas to hold the rain and to

145

disperse the frost. They say tobacco is the thirteen-month crop, and the labors of January are only the beginning.

Maggie Ledford Lawson has written of her girlhood in Hawkins County. Married in August, three days before her fifteenth birthday, she learned the following winter to accept the role of a mountain wife. "Every morning around five, I get up and hurry over cold linoleum to the kitchen, where I lay hickory kindling, then larger sticks of oak or pine, in the narrow iron grate of the cookstove. The fire going, I hurry back to bed to crawl under a heavy homemade quilt. For a half hour I can stay in that snug cocoon, resisting the metamorphosis of a winter morning, then duty calls from cold linoleum again. There are biscuits to be made, rounded and soft on top, brown at the edges. We have no refrigerator, but that's no problem: the milk in the kitchen is always ringed with an inch of icy mush. Our Guernsey, Stuck-in-the-Mud, has to be coaxed from a pawpaw thicket. Her brushy tail is thick with icy needles, and she flails it in my face to add to the sunrise pleasures. At last I go back to the kitchen with a pail nearly full of warm and foamy milk."

Hard lines, these, but the isolation of the mountains creates intense bonds between mountain people and the animals they live with. Every household has at least one dog, often a 'coon hound whose built-in bagpipes can make the hillside ring by night. Our barn cats are as streetwise as the dudes of Harlem; they live by their wits and feed on field mice. In Virginia, Kentucky, and Maryland especially, but in parts of Louisiana and Florida also, riding horses rank as members of the family. Mules tend to be tolerated with the exasperated affection reserved for old and eccentric uncles.

Animals are more than companions and co-workers. Game biologists believe there are more deer in Virginia now than there were when John Smith came to Jamestown. Over most of the South squirrels and rabbits abound. They provide important supplements to the food supply. The trapping of muskrat and beaver still figures here and there in farm income. Skunks, foxes, groundhogs, bears, and bobcats manage to coexist in our woodlands.

And birds! Up in the Dakotas, the rocket rise of a ringneck pheasant is a beautiful thing to behold, but it cannot compare to the awesome entrance of a wild turkey on the wing. These magnificent birds are as big as B-52s, and when three or four come together down a glade it is like a stately procession within the House of Lords. For some years it was feared the turkey might become extinct, but careful game management has reversed a long and ominous trend.

Hunters in the Carolinas never tire of quail hunting, and fortunately the quail never tire of replenishing their coveys. I myself won't hunt them: They are too much fun to watch. Quail will waddle down country lanes as puffed-up as so many Richmond dowagers, ignoring the "walk" and "don't walk" signals, window shopping the ditch-banks as they go. Many Southern farms have house coveys, tame as chickens, that will come to bird feeders off and on throughout a winter day. They lunch on the seeds and cracked corn scratched down by the blue jays. I once counted twenty-four of them outside my office window, racked up together like billiard balls. Out in the field, they scatter in explosions of brown and white. On a Sunday morning table, nested in bacon, they provide an unbeatable brunch.

The smell of woodsmoke, the contemplative joys of a kitchen fire, a cardinal's Christmas ribbon flight—these are among the things we love. But Southern winters, outside the balmy climes of Florida, are not really to be highly recommended. They provide moments of frozen beauty, as William Bake's photographs will tell us, but they are more to be tolerated than embraced. The best that can be said of them, echoing Mr. Shelley, is that when a Southern winter comes, a Southern spring cannot be far behind.

High January.
RICH MOUNTAIN, NORTH CAROLINA.

148

Winter Dusk on Shenandoah Street. HARPERS FERRY, WEST VIRGINIA.

Snowswept Cemetery. HARPERS FERRY, WEST VIRGINIA.

Above Boone. WATAUGA COUNTY, NORTH CAROLINA.

152

Winter Passage. POND MOUNTAIN, TENNESSEE.

Storm Aftermath.
OCONEE COUNTY, GEORGIA.

Dockside at Day's End. ST. MARYS, GEORGIA.

Haiku Transposed. OKEFENOKEE NATIONAL WILDLIFE REFUGE, GEORGIA.

Sea Wind, Approaching Storm. CUMBERLAND ISLAND NATIONAL SEASHORE, GEORGIA.

158

Kraft Mill. ST. MARYS, GEORGIA.

Double Shoals on the Apalachee.
MORGAN COUNTY, GEORGIA.

Spanish Moss. OKEFENOKEE NATIONAL WILDLIFE REFUGE, GEORGIA.

Dungeness. CUMBERLAND ISLAND NATIONAL SEASHORE, GEORGIA.

Waiting Out the Afternoon.
SAVANNAH, GEORGIA.

Silhouette at Sunset. ST. MARYS, GEORGIA.

162

Secured for the Night. BEAUFORT, SOUTH CAROLINA.

Lamplight at Hibernian Hall. CHARLESTON, SOUTH CAROLINA.

Battery Rooftops.
CHARLESTON, SOUTH CAROLINA.

164

Quiet Afternoon Along the Kiawah. KIAWAH RIVER, SOUTH CAROLINA.

The Marshes of Glynn.
ST. MARYS, GEORGIA.

The Joseph Johnson House (c. 1850).
BEAUFORT, SOUTH CAROLINA.

Caretaker's Liberty.
CHARLESTON, SOUTH CAROLINA.

Interior: The Oldest House. ST. AUGUSTINE, FLORIDA.

Cable House; Winter Rain.
GREAT SMOKY MOUNTAINS
NATIONAL PARK, TENNESSEE.

White Dune and Lichens. GULF SHORES, ALABAMA.

Bunch's Store. KINGSTON, ARKANSAS.

173

The Pontalba at Jackson Square. NEW ORLEANS, LOUSIANA.

The Forager. Wichita Mountains Wildlife Refuge, Oklahoma.

Comanche Territory.
Wichita Mountains Wildlife Refuge, Oklahoma.

174

The Old Greer County Hall of Fame. MANGUM, OKLAHOMA.

176

Eras Meet. UMBARGER, TEXAS.

High Plains Church. VALENTINE, TEXAS.

Panhandle Farmhouse. HAPPY, TEXAS.

Juniper Canyon. BIG BEND NATIONAL PARK, TEXAS.

Prairie Dog Town Fork, The Red River. PALO DURO CANYON STATE PARK, TEXAS.

Clearing Skies Over North Mountain. Hueco Tanks State Park, Texas.

High Plains Storm. CORNUDAS, TEXAS.

Mission Socorro. EL PASO, TEXAS.

Arizona Oaks.
HUECO TANKS STATE PARK, TEXAS.

Santa Elena Canyon.
Big Bend National Park, Texas.

Reprise: The Seasons. HARPERS FERRY, WEST VIRGINIA.

THE AMERICAN SOUTH
Four Seasons of the Land

Designed by Robert L. Nance

Text composed in Linotron Optima by
Akra Data, Inc., Birmingham, Alabama

Color separations by
Capitol Engraving Company, Nashville, Tennessee

Text paper is Lustro Offset Enamel Dull by
The S. D. Warren Company, Boston, Massachusetts

Endleaves are Rhododendron Text, Telanian Finish, by
Strathmore Paper Company, Westfield, Massachusetts

Cover cloth is Record Buckram by
The Holliston Mills, Inc., Kingsport, Tennessee

Printed and Bound by
Kingsport Press Inc., Kingsport, Tennessee

27